Karl
Jenkins

THE PEACEMAKERS

for chorus & ensemble

VOCAL SCORE

T0066569

BOOSEY & HAWKES

Boosey & Hawkes Music Publishers Ltd
www.boosey.com

Published by Boosey & Hawkes Music Publishers Ltd
Aldwych House
71–91 Aldwych
London
WC2B 4HN

www.boosey.com

AN IMAGEM COMPANY

I offer you peace
Words attributed to M K Gandhi used with permission of the M K Gandhi Institute for Non Violence:
www.gandhiinstitute.org

Inner Peace
Words from His Holiness the 14th Dalai Lama of Tibet used with permission of the Office of His Holiness
the Dalai Lama: www.dalailama.com

Meditation: Peace is …
Text © copyright 2011 by Terry Waite. Reproduced by permission.

Fiat pax in virtute tua
Mother Teresa's words used with permission of the Mother Teresa Center: www.motherteresa.org
Words attributed to Albert Schweitzer (1875–1965), philosopher, theologian, organist and medical doctor.
Used with permission: www.albertschweitzer.org.uk

Let there be justice for all
Words by Nelson Mandela used by permission of the Nelson Mandela Foundation:
www.nelsonmandela.org

Anthem: Peace, triumphant peace
Words by Anne Frank used with permission of Anne Frank Stichting – Anne Frank House:
www.annefrank.org

ISMN 979-0-060-12434-1
ISBN 978-0-85162-696-3

First printed 2012. Fifth impression 2015

Printed by Halstan:
Halstan UK, 2–10 Plantation Road, Amersham, Bucks, HP6 6HJ. United Kingdom
Halstan DE, Weißliliengasse 4, 55116 Mainz. Germany

Cover image courtesy of Warner Classics
www.warnerclassics.com

Photo credits
Dalai Lama: D Dipasupil/FilmMagic/Getty Images
Gandhi: AFP/Getty Images
Martin Luther King: Martin Mills/Getty Images
Nelson Mandela: Trevor Samson/AFP/Getty Images
Mother Teresa: Ron Galella/WireImage
Karl Jenkins: Rhys Frampton

Music origination by Jon Bunker

CONTENTS

Preface v

Text vi

Scoring x

Performance notes xi

First recording details xii

THE PEACEMAKERS

Part I

1   Blessed are the peacemakers 1

2   Fanfara 6

3   Peace, peace! 20

4   I offer your peace 25

5   Inner peace 32

6   Healing Light: a Celtic prayer 37

7   Meditation: Peace is 45

8   Evening Prayer 48

Intermezzo

9   Solitude (*optional – voices tacet*)

Part II

10   Fiat pax in virtute tua 58

11   He had a dream *Elegy for Martin Luther King Jr* 66

12   The Dove 72

13   The Peace Prayer of St Francis of Assisi 77

14   One Song 85

15   Let there be justice for all 98

16   Dona nobis pacem 106

17   Anthem: Peace, triumphant peace 116

'Music has the capacity to breathe harmony into the soul.
The Peacemakers breathes the harmony of peace.'

Terry Waite CBE

'*The Peacemakers* is dedicated to the memory of all those who lost
their lives during armed conflict: in particular, innocent civilians.
When I composed *The Armed Man: A Mass for Peace* for the
millennium, it was with the hope of looking forward to
a century of peace. Sadly, nothing much has changed.'

Karl Jenkins CBE

PREFACE

The Peacemakers is a work extolling peace. One line, from Rumi (the 13th-century Persian mystic poet whose words I have set) sums up the ethos of the piece: 'All religions, all singing one song: Peace be with you'. Many of the 'contributors' are iconic figures that have shaped history, others are less well known. I have occasionally placed some text in a musical environment that helps identify their origin or culture; the bansuri (Indian flute) and tabla in the Gandhi, the shakuhachi (a Japanese flute associated with Zen Buddhism) and temple bells in that of the Dalai Lama, African percussion in the Mandela and echoes of the blues of the deep American South (as well as a quote from Schumann's *Träumerei* (Dreaming) in my tribute to Martin Luther King. 'Healing Light: a Celtic prayer' is just that, with uilleann pipes and bodhrán drums. I have also presented some odd combinations, such as 'monastic chant meets the ethnic' in 'Let there be justice for all' and 'Inner peace'.

Having decided on *The Peacemakers* as the textual core and title of my new work the search was on to find messengers of peace. A handful of obvious figures came to mind, figures that have changed the world, such as Gandhi, Mandela and Martin Luther King, followed by such iconic and inspiring people as Mother Teresa and Anne Frank. Having sourced suitable and pithy text from these the net was cast to find other 'peacemakers'. I had been aware of Albert Schweitzer as a boy, in part because my organist father had recordings of him playing Bach, and I had previously set the Persian mystic poet, Rumi, in my *Stabat Mater*. I felt I needed something from the Abrahamic religions, so there are words from Christ, the Qur'an, Judaism and St Seraphim of Sarov (a Russian Orthodox monk), while St Francis of Assisi is included by association. I also quote from the Old Testament Book of Isaiah in my homage to Martin Luther King, as he did in his 'I have a dream' speech. English poets, Shelley and Malory are heard, as is Bahá'u'lláh, the founder of the Bahá'í faith. Carol Barratt added further text with the odd sentence from me. Some anonymous traditional text has also been included. I feel privileged that Terry Waite CBE has contributed some wonderful words, especially written for *The Peacemakers*.

Karl Jenkins
September 2011

The Peacemakers

Part I

1 – Blessed are the peacemakers

Blessed are the Peacemakers for they will be called the children of God.

Jesus Christ – Matthew 5: 9

Shalom. Shanti. Salam.

'Peace' in Hebrew, Hindi and Arabic

2 – Fanfara

'Peace' in various languages:

Frieden *German*
Mir *Russian*
Peace *English*
Pace *Italian*
Pax *Latin*
He ping *Mandarin*
Heddwch *Welsh*
Heiwa *Japanese*
Shanti *Hindi*
Paz *Spanish*
Paix *French*
Shalom *Hebrew*
Salam *Arabic*
Aramaic *Shlamah*
Selam *Ethiopian*
Rauha *Finnish*
Irini *Greek*
Vrede *Dutch*
Béke *Hungarian*
Fred *Swedish*
Pokój *Polish*

3 – Peace, peace!

Peace, peace! he is not dead, he doth not sleep –
He hath awakened from the dream of life –
'Tis we, who lost in stormy visions, keep
With phantoms an unprofitable strife.

Percy Bysshe Shelley (1792–1822), from Elegy on the Death of John Keats

Shelley was considered to be one of the greatest English Romantic poets. He met his death by drowning off the coast of Italy.

Shalom. Shanti. Shlama. Salam.

'Peace' in Hebrew, Hindi, Aramaic and Arabic

4 – I offer you peace

I offer you peace. I offer you love. I offer you friendship. I see your beauty. I hear your need. I feel your feelings. My wisdom flows from the Highest Source. I salute that Source in you. Let us work together for unity and love … an eye for an eye leaves the whole world blind.

Words attributed to Mahatma Gandhi, 1869–1948

A pioneer of non-violent civil disobedience as political protest, Mohandas Karamchand Gandhi was the leader of the Indian nationalist struggle for independence. A thinker and prolific writer on the concept of non-violence, he was assassinated in Delhi on 30 January 1948.

5 – Inner peace

We can never have peace in the world if we neglect the inner world and don't make peace with ourselves. World peace must develop out of inner peace.

Peace starts within each one of us. When we have inner peace we can be at peace with those around us.

His Holiness the 14th Dalai Lama of Tibet (b 1935)

The 14th Dalai Lama (Tenzin Gyatso) is the spiritual leader of Tibetan Buddhism. Dalai Lamas are believed by followers of Buddhism to be reincarnations of previous holders of the title, a tradition dating back to the 15th century. The current Dalai Lama won the Nobel Prize for Peace in 1989 for his 'efforts for a peaceful resolution' in the struggle for Tibetan independence.

6 – Healing Light: a Celtic prayer

Deep peace of the running wave to you,
Deep peace of the flowing air to you,
Deep peace of the quiet earth to you,
Deep peace of the shining stars to you,
Deep peace of the gentle night to you,
Moon and stars pour their healing light on you,
Deep peace of Christ, the light of the world,
   to you,
Deep peace of Christ to you.
Amen.

Anon

7 – Meditation: Peace is …

Peace is the fragile meeting
Of two souls in harmony.

Peace is an embrace
That protects and heals.

Peace is a reconciling
Of opposites.

Peace is rooted in love,
It lies in the heart
Waiting to be nourished,
Blossom
And flourish
Until it embraces the world.

May we know the harmony of peace.
May we sing the harmony of peace.
Until in the last of days
We rest in peace.

Terry Waite CBE (b 1939) was a special envoy to the Archbishop of Canterbury when, in January 1987, he was captured by terrorists in Beirut while attempting to secure the release of hostages. He was held captive for nearly five years.

8 – Evening Prayer

Matthew, Mark, Luke and John,
Bless this bed that I lie on.
Before I lay me down to sleep,
I pray the Lord my soul to keep.

Four corners to my bed,
Four angels there are spread;
Two at the foot, two at the head:
Four to carry me when I'm dead.

I go by sea, I go by land:
The Lord made me with his right hand.
Should any danger come to me,
Sweet Jesus Christ deliver me.

He's my branch and I'm the flower,
Pray God send me a happy hour;
And should I die before I wake,
I pray the Lord my soul to take.

Anon

Intermezzo
9 – Solitude *Solo violin & strings*

Part II

10 – Fiat pax in virtute tua

Fiat pax in virtute tua et abundantia in turribus tuis.
Propter fratres meos et proximos meos loquebar pacem de te.

Psalm 122: 7–8 (English translation is shown below where it is sung)

Peace begins with a smile. If we have no peace, it is because we have forgotten that we belong to each other.

Mother Teresa (1910–97)

Mother Teresa of Calcutta founded the Missionaries of Charity in 1950. In recognition of her dedication to helping the poor and sick she was awarded the Nobel Prize for Peace and the Bharat Ratna (India's highest civilian honour). She was beatified by Pope John Paul II in 2003.

Peace be within thy walls and prosperity within thy palaces.
For my brethren and companions' sakes I will now say, Peace be within thee.

Psalm 122: 7–8

The important thing in life is the traces of love that we leave behind when we have to leave unasked and say farewell.

Albert Schweitzer, 1875–1965

Schweitzer was a renowned German theologian, philosopher and humanitarian, and was awarded the Nobel Prize for Peace in 1952. As an organist and musicologist he is noted for his research into the life of J S Bach.

And the true servants of the All-Merciful walk the earth with humility, and when the ignorant address them they say, 'Peace'.

Qur'an 25: 63

11 – He had a dream
Elegy for Martin Luther King Jr

He had a dream that all mankind could live together in peace and harmony.
He had a dream that people of different colours and creeds could live together.
He had a dream that …

Karl Jenkins

... every valley shall be exalted, every mountain and hill shall be made low: and the crooked shall be made straight, and the rough places plain. And the glory of the Lord shall be revealed, and all flesh shall see it together.

Isaiah 40: 4–5

That was his dream. He had a dream.

Born in 1929, Martin Luther King Jr was an American clergyman who played a major role in the African-American civil rights movement, using methods of peaceful protest inspired by the teachings of Mahatma Gandhi. In 1964, aged just 35, he became the youngest person to be awarded the Nobel Prize for Peace. He was shot dead in Memphis, Tennessee, on 4 April 1968 and is remembered today as an icon in the campaign for civil rights, both in the United States and worldwide.

12 – The Dove
for Astrid May

Dove of peace fly here to find us,
Feathers softly stroking the earth.
Dove of peace so soft, so silent,
Please protect each innocent birth.

Dove of peace we reach to touch you,
Pure and white, please comfort our fears.
Spread contentment gently near us,
Spread your wings and dry all our tears.

Dove of peace fly here to find us,
Feathers caught in circles of light.
Dove of peace so soft, so silent,
Turn each day to sweet sleep each night.

Carol Barratt

13 – The Peace Prayer of St Francis of Assisi

O Lord, make me an instrument of thy peace,
where there is hatred, let me sow love;
where there is injury, pardon;
where there is discord, harmony;
where there is doubt, faith;
where there is despair, hope;
where there is darkness, light;
where there is sorrow, joy.

O Divine Master, grant that I may not so
   much seek
to be consoled as to console;
to be understood as to understand;

to be loved as to love;
it is in pardoning that we are pardoned;
it is in dying that we are born to eternal life.

St Francis of Assisi was born in 1181 or 1182. A friar and preacher who founded the Franciscan Order of monks, he died in 1226 and was canonised by Pope Gregory IX two years later. Nowadays he is known as the patron saint of animals and is one of the most esteemed religious leaders in history. This text is closely associated with St Francis, but it was in fact written anonymously and first appeared in 1912 in France.

14 – One Song

No more war, ...

Karl Jenkins

... better is peace than always war, better is peace than ever more war.

Sir Thomas Malory (1405–71), English writer and poet, from Le morte d'Arthur

All religions. All this singing. One song.
Peace be with you.

Rumi (1207–73), Persian Muslim cleric and mystic poet

Blessed peace, blessed peace, take away
   torment and be at peace.
Please make our future a world without war.
Give us a future that we can call our own.
Grant us a life where love and peace
   surround us.
Bended knees, folded hands, listen to prayers
from many lands.
Crying for mercy and pleading for peace.
Shalom.
Sing one song, sing peace be with you.
Give us a future free from dark despair.
Pilgrims who take the light of the world to share.
No more war, no more war.

Carol Barratt / Karl Jenkins

15 – Let there be justice for all

After climbing a great hill one finds that there are many more hills to climb. I have taken a moment here to rest, to steal a view of the glorious vista that surrounds me, to look back on the distance I have come. But I can rest only for a moment, for with freedom come responsibilities, and I dare not linger, for my long walk is not yet ended.

Let there be justice for all. Let there be peace for all. Let there be work, bread, water and salt for all. Let each know that for each the body, the mind and the soul have been freed to fulfil themselves.

Nelson Mandela (b 1918), from The Long Walk to Freedom *(1995)*

Nelson Mandela organised protest against South Africa's apartheid regime and was jailed for 27 years. Freed in February 1990, he won the Nobel Prize for Peace in 1993 and was appointed South Africa's first black president in 1994.

16 – Dona nobis pacem

Lord give us peace.
Dona nobis pacem.

Ordinary of the Mass

The world is but one country, and mankind its citizens. We are all fruits of one tree and leaves of one branch.

Bahá'u'lláh (1817–92)

Born in Tehran, Bahá'u'lláh was the founder of the Bahá'í faith. Bahá'í teaches the unity of God, the unity of religion and the unity of humankind. Bahá'u'lláh's claim to divine revelation resulted in 40 years of persecution and imprisonment. He died within the prison city of 'Akka, Palestine (Acre in present-day Israel).

17 – Anthem: Peace, triumphant peace

Peace, triumphant peace shall reign on Earth some day.
Pray for peace and make your words echo round the world for peace one day, on Earth one day, that wondrous day when the world has peace, glorious peace, such peace.

When will such lasting peace arrive on that wondrous day on this our Earth?
May all our paths meet up and lead to one holy place where peace shall reign in our hearts, one wondrous day when the world has peace, glorious peace, such peace.

Carol Barratt

How wonderful it is that no-one need wait a single moment before starting to improve the world.

Anne Frank (1929–45)

Anne Frank, born in Frankfurt, was a Jewish victim of Nazi persecution. Following the German occupation of the Netherlands her family went into hiding in a secret annexe at her father's office in Amsterdam. After two years they were betrayed. She kept a diary of this period which has been translated into more than 55 languages. Anne Frank died of typhus in the Bergen-Belsen concentration camp.

Embrace the spirit of peace and thousands of souls around you will be saved.

St Seraphim of Sarov (1759–1833)

St Seraphim of Sarov became a monk of the Russian Orthodox Church at the age of 19. He lived as a hermit and received thousands of pilgrims. He was renowned for his ascetic life, his wisdom, gifts of healing and powers of prophecy.

SCORING

SATB chorus
optional Chorus II (upper voices)

Instrumentation

Flute (doubling Piccolo and optional Bass Flute)
5-string Fretless Bass Guitar (or Classical or Acoustic Guitar)
Percussion (3)★
Strings

★'Ethnic' percussion

2 low Floor Tom-toms (different tensions)
Goblet Drum (*eg* Darbuca, Tablas, Bodhrán)
Tambourim
Pandeiro or Riq (Tambourine may be substituted)
Bamboo Chimes
Mark Tree

Standard percussion

Glockenspiel
Crotales
Tubular Bells
Marimba
2 Tuned Bells (E, B – see performance notes)
Triangle
Snare Drum
Tenor Drum
Bass Drum
Tam-tam (low)
Cymbals
Suspended Cymbal

Optional instruments

Descant Recorder(s)
Tin Whistle
Uilleann Pipes
Soprano Saxophone
3 Trumpets in B♭
3 Tenor Trombones
Bass Trombone
Tuba
Timpani
Solo Violin
Organ or Electronic Keyboard (doubling Celesta)

PERFORMANCE NOTES

1. The overall 'choral sing' is the same length as for *The Armed Man*.

2. 'Solitude' may be omitted.

3. The work may be sung in one complete movement or in two halves.

4. Although several *ethnic* flutes are employed on the recording all such parts can be played on a normal concert flute.

5. In the absence of fretless bass guitar the part may be played on classical or acoustic guitar.

6. The score is constructed so that the whole work may be sung by an SATB choir, without Chorus II. If used, Chorus II should comprise children or young people with unbroken voices: they should not sound like adults.

7. Instrumentation is listed overleaf. The recording is scored for strings, brass, organ and percussion. The brass and organ are optional and are only used for the louder movements and passages to add weight and drama. It is recommended that at least a keyboard (with organ tone) be employed, in which case the player should play the right hand material and either left hand or pedal (the latter in octaves) depending on the strength of the string section in the ensemble. Celesta is in any case optional. All brass should be used or none at all.

8. In 'Healing Light' the passages for tin whistle and uilleann pipes can be played by the flautist on piccolo or treble recorder. Other possibilities include: acoustic guitar on its own or with soprano saxophone; children's recorder group.

9. To support the long sections of *a cappella* singing, optional string accompaniment is included in the score and parts.

10. Regarding the optional saxophone part it is advisable, since improvisation is involved, that it be omitted if the performer is not of the highest quality.

11. Percussion, player 1: apart from in movement 2 ('Fanfara'), this part involves specialist 'hand' and 'ethnic' drumming improvisatory parts. Even so, there remain two highly specialised instruments in the score (Irish bodhrán and Indian tablas) that may be simulated by using a goblet drum (*eg* darbuca).

12. Percussion, players 2 and 3 play standard orchestral percussion and can interchange parts. The tuned bells represent Buddhist temple bells; hand-bells may be used but since the dynamic is *piano* the bells should be mounted and struck, not played with the clapper.

The Peacemakers was first performed on 16 January 2012 at Carnegie Hall, New York,
by Distinguished Concerts International New York (DCINY).
This performance in support of GlobalSingforPeace.org

Antoni Mendezona (soprano), Jorge Avila (violin),
Kara DeRaad Santos (flutes), Premik Russell Tubbs (bansuri and ethnic flutes),
Joseph Mulvanerty (uilleann pipes), Rob Derke, NYJAZZ (soprano saxophone),
Carlo De Rosa, NYJAZZ (fretless bass guitar),
Benny Koonyevsky, NYJAZZ (ethnic percussion)

Distinguished Concerts Singers International★

★Blythewood High School Choir (SC), Choir18 (MD),
The Choristers of All Saints, Phoenix (AZ), Coleytown Middle School Camerata (CT),
Dedham Choral Society (MA), Guernsey Choral & Orchestral Society (UK),
Hilo Community Chorus (HI), Manhattan School of Music (NY),
Die Meistersingers and Il Bel Canto (MD), Metropolitan Detroit Chorale (MI),
Musica Antigua Collegii (Australia), The Really Big Chorus (UK),
Sine Nomine Singers (NC), Vocal Spotlight (OH)

Distinguished Concerts Orchestra International

Conducted by Karl Jenkins

Prepared by Jonathan Griffith

First recording: EMI CD 50999 0 84378 2 2

Lucy Crowe (soprano), Chloë Hanslip (violin),
Gareth Davies (flutes), Ashwin Shrinivasan (bansuri), Clive Bell (shakuhachi),
Davy Spillane (uilleann pipes), Nigel Hitchcock (soprano saxophone),
Laurence Cottle (fretless bass guitar), Jody K Jenkins (ethnic percussion)

Rundfunkchor Berlin and the
City of Birmingham Symphony Orchestra Youth Chorus,
chorus master Simon Halsey

The Really Big Chorus†

†The Angmering Chorale, Ashtead Choral Society,
Beckenham Chorale, Billingshurst Choral Society, Burgess Hill Choral Society,
Camerata Chamber Choir Isle of Wight, Carshalton Choral Society & Holy Cross Choir,
Gainsborough Choral Society, Havering Singers, Hook Choral Society,
Leatherhead Choral Society, Leicester Philharmonic Choir,
Redland Green Community Chorus,
St James's Church Choir, Finchampstead,
the Tyranno Chorus

London Symphony Orchestra (Carmine Lauri, leader)

Conducted by Karl Jenkins

THE PEACEMAKERS

THE PEACEMAKERS
Part I

1 – Blessed are the peacemakers

MATTHEW 5: 9

KARL JENKINS

★See performance notes.

19260

peace-ma - kers, for___ they will__ be_ called___ the child - ren of

peace - ma - kers, for__ they will be called the child - ren of

peace - ma - kers, for they will be called the child - ren of

peace - ma - kers, for they will be called the child - ren of

God,_____ God,__ the child-ren of

God,____ God,__ the child-ren of

God,____ God,__ the child-ren of

God,_____ God,__ the child - ren of

4

5

9260

2 – Fanfara

Text: 'peace' in
various languages

KARL JENKINS

★TB divide equally in 3 where divisi occur

19260

12

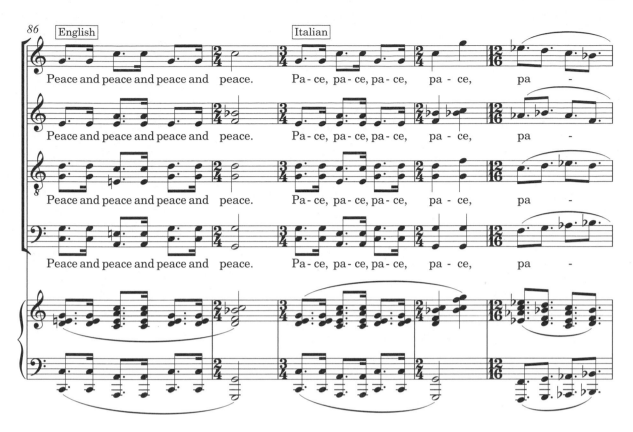

18

19260

3 – Peace, peace!

PERCY BYSSHE SHELLEY

KARL JENKINS

★See performance notes. In this movement Chorus II may be omitted altogether as its material is doubled by Trumpet 1.

© Copyright 2011 by Boosey & Hawkes Music Publishers Ltd

19260

24

19260

4 – I offer you peace

MAHATMA GANDHI

KARL JENKINS

19260

see_____ your beau-ty._____ I_ hear_____ your need._____ I_ feel_____ your

see_____ your beau-ty._____ I_ hear_____ your need._____ I_ feel_____ your

Ch II

feel-ings._____ My_ wis - dom flows from the High - est Source. I sa - lute that Source in

S

feel-ings._____ My_ wis - dom flows from the High - est Source. I sa - lute that Source in

A

Sing if no Chorus II

My_ wis - dom flows from the High - est Source. I sa-lute that Source in

36
let us work to - ge - ther for u - ni - ty and love.
whole world blind.
whole world blind.
whole world blind.
whole world blind.
B
40
p
I of - fer you peace. I
Sing if no Chorus II
p
I of - fer you peace. I
B
p

5 – Inner peace

THE DALAI LAMA

KARL JENKINS

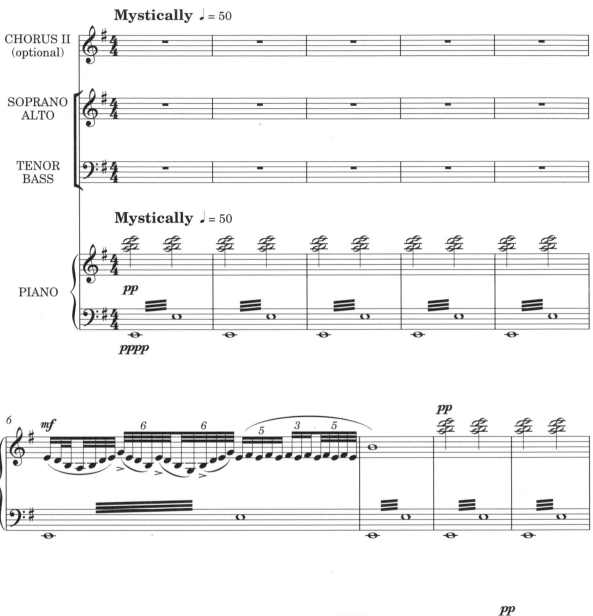

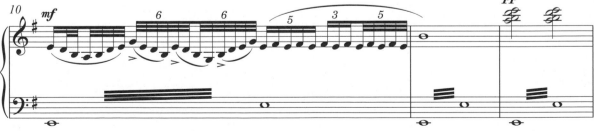

19260

in - ner peace, in - - - ner peace.

in - ner peace, in - - - ner peace.

in - ner peace, in - - - ner peace.

in - ner peace, in - - - ner peace.

in - ner peace, in - - - ner peace.

6 – Healing Light: a Celtic prayer

ANON

KARL JENKINS

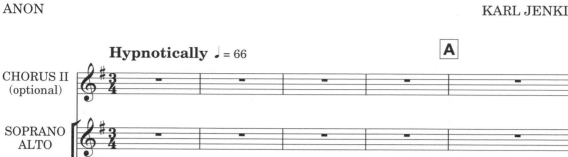

19260

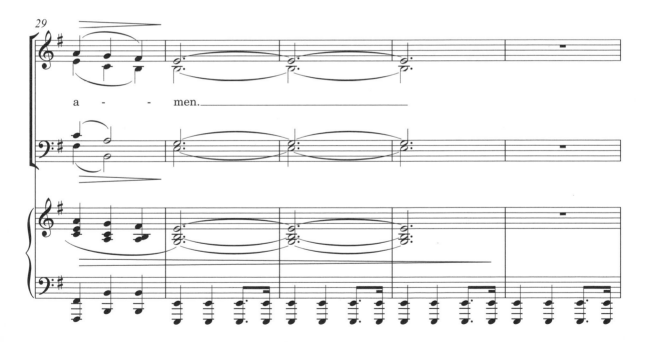

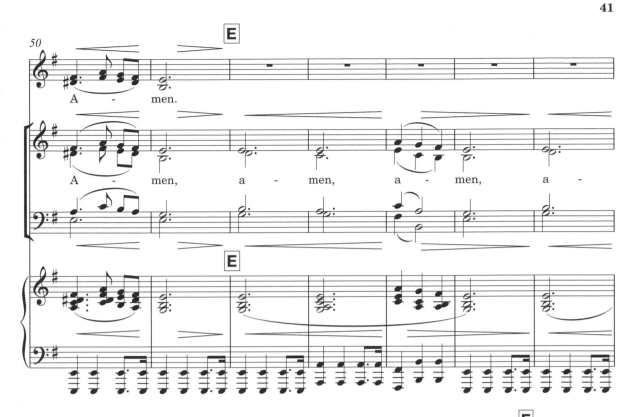

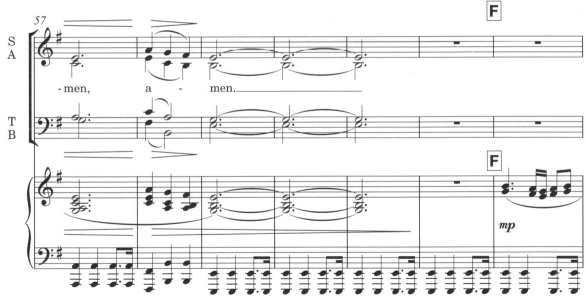

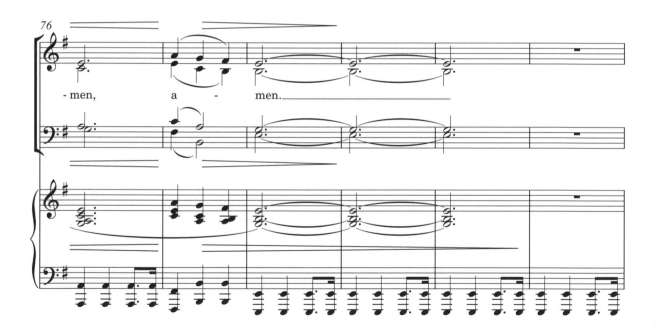

a - men, a - men, a - men,

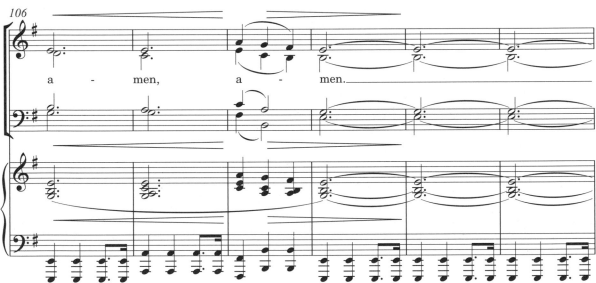

a - men, a - men.

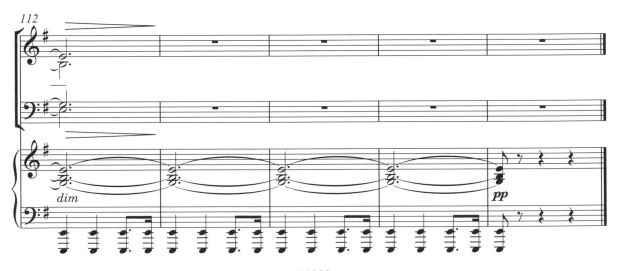

dim

pp

7 – Meditation: Peace is …

TERRY WAITE

KARL JENKINS

19260

Peace is a re-con-cil-ing Of op - po-sites.___

Peace is root-ed in love,___ It lies___ in the heart___

Wait - ing to be nour-ished, Blos - som And flour - ish,

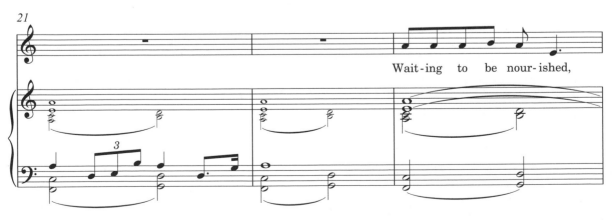

Wait - ing to be nour-ished,

8 – Evening Prayer

ANON

KARL JENKINS

Innocently ♩ = 120

PIANO

A

Ch II

Mat - thew, Mark, Luke and John, Bless this bed that I lie

Sing only if no Chorus II

S A

Mat - thew, Mark, Luke and John, Bless this bed that I lie

19260

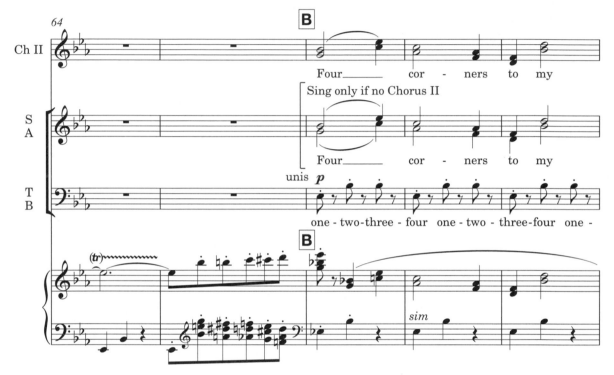

two at the head: Four to car - ry me when I'm dead.

two at the head: Four to car - ry me when I'm dead, Four to

one - two one - two one - two

S
A

car - ry me when I'm dead.

T
B

★If no Chorus II then Chorus I sopranos divide to cover both soprano parts.

soul to take, I pray the Lord my soul

soul to take, I pray the Lord my soul

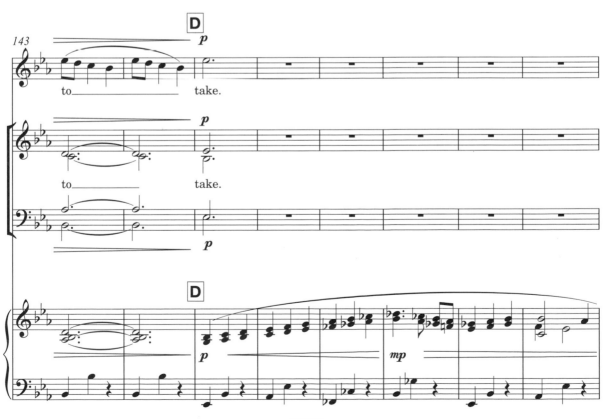

to take.

to take.

56

19260

Lyrics under the music: John. bless_ this bed that I lie on.

Intermezzo

9 – Solitude
(optional movement)

VOICES TACET

Part II
10 – Fiat pax in virtute tua

PSALM 122: 7–8;
MOTHER TERESA;
ALBERT SCHWEITZER;
QUR'AN 25: 63

KARL JENKINS

19260

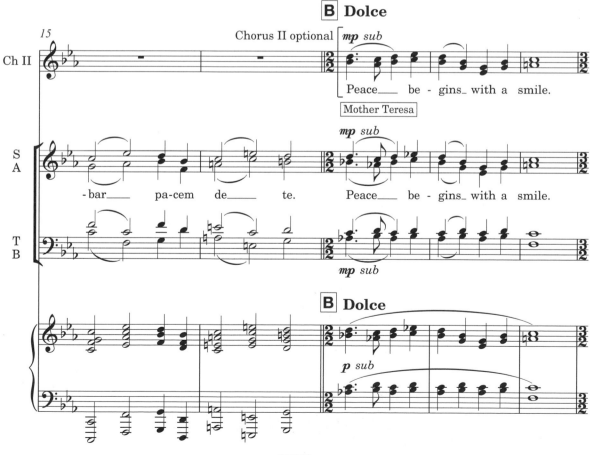

20

If____ we have no peace it____ is be-cause we have for - got - ten that__ we be-

If____ we have no peace it____ is be-cause we have for - got - ten that__ we be-

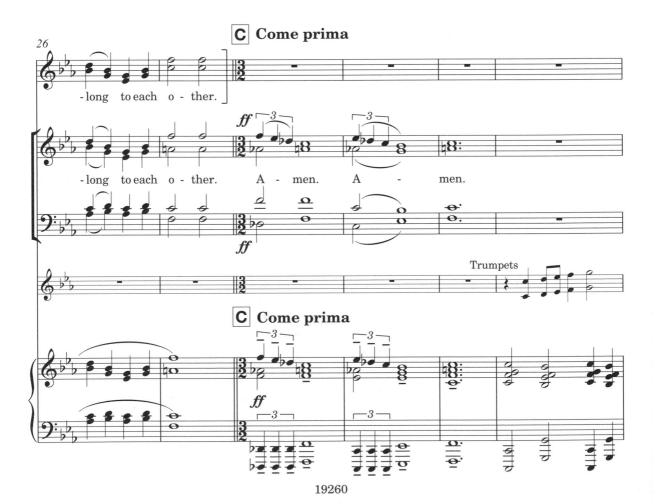

26

C **Come prima**

-long to each o - ther.

-long to each o - ther. A - men. A - men.

Trumpets

C **Come prima**

66

11 – He had a dream

Elegy for Martin Luther King Jr

KARL JENKINS;
ISAIAH 40: 4–5

KARL JENKINS

19260

68

19260

Träumerei (Dreaming) – Schumann

for Astrid May

12 – The Dove

CAROL BARRATT

KARL JENKINS

★Solo voice may be a child or adult female.

19260

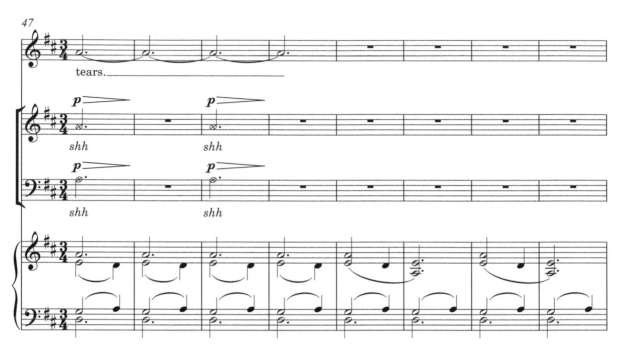

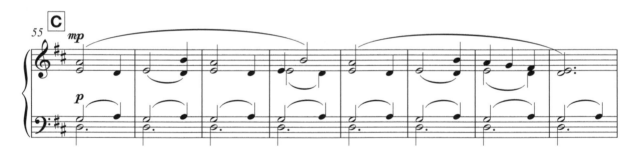

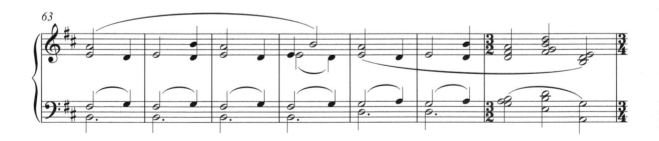

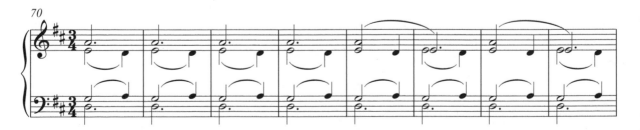

13 – The Peace Prayer of St Francis of Assisi

ANON

KARL JENKINS

19260

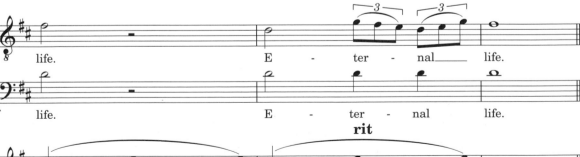

14 – One Song

SIR THOMAS MALORY; RUMI;
CAROL BARRATT; KARL JENKINS

KARL JENKINS

19260

★Lowest part may be omitted.   19260

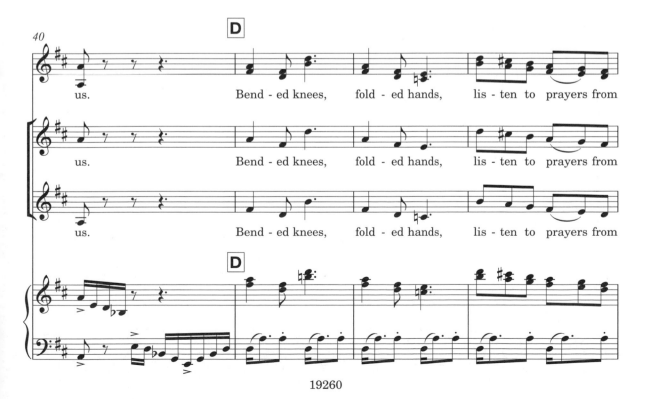

E If no improvised solo, E – F may be cut.

Sing one song, one song, one song, sing

Sing one song, one song, one song, sing

E If no improvised solo, E – F may be cut.

peace be with you. Sing one song, one song, one song, sing

peace be with you. Sing one song, one song, one song, sing

94

★Lowest part may be omitted.

15 – Let there be justice for all

NELSON MANDELA

KARL JENKINS

Words by Nelson Mandela, used by permission of the Nelson Mandela Foundation:
www.nelsonmandela.org

19260

16 – Dona nobis pacem

TRAD; BAHÁ'U'LLÁH

KARL JENKINS

19260

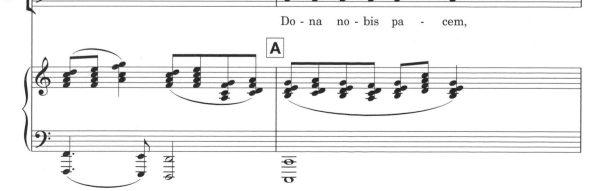

★If no Chorus II then this is sung by a semichorus taken from Chorus I.

★If no Chorus II then Flute plays this passage to the end.

17 – Anthem: Peace, triumphant peace

CAROL BARRATT;
ANNE FRANK;
ST SERAPHIM OF SAROV

KARL JENKINS

19260

7 (22)

Earth some day.
this our Earth?

Pray, pray for peace and make your words e - cho round the world for
May all our paths meet up and lead to one ho - ly place where

10 (25)

peace one day, on Earth one__ day, that won-drous day when the world has__
peace shall reign, shall reign in our hearts, one won-drous day when the world has__

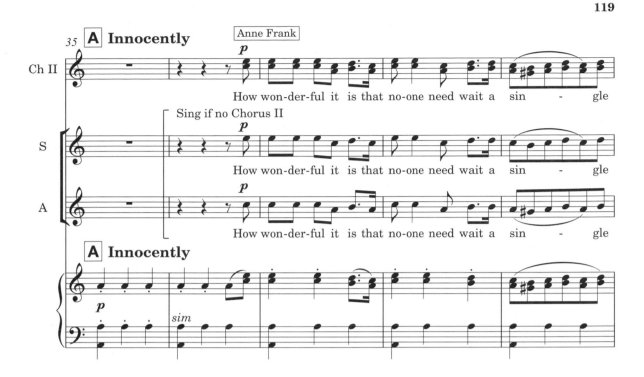

122

19260

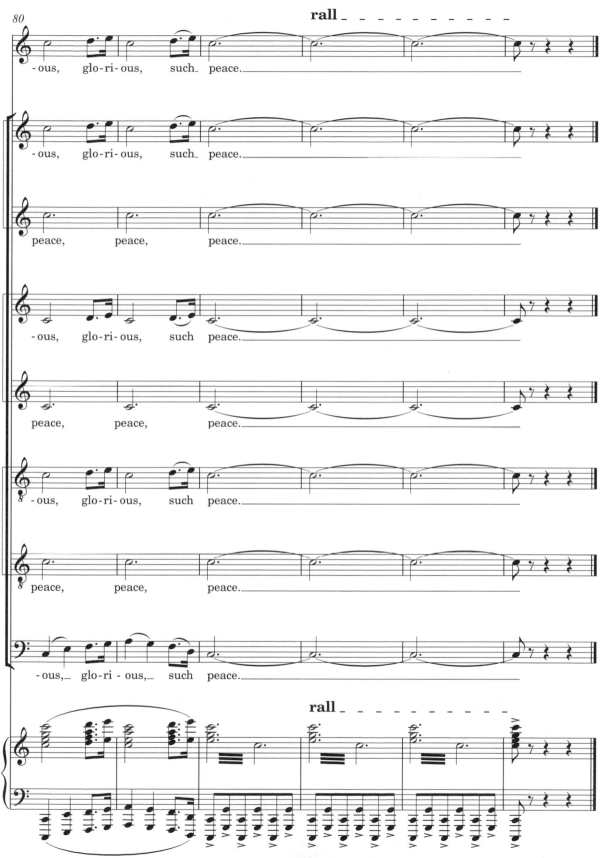

Works for chorus & orchestra by Karl Jenkins

Stabat Mater
Vocal score (Contralto solo, SATB & piano)
ISMN: 979-0-060-11952-1

Gloria
Vocal score (Solo voice, SATB & piano)
ISMN: 979-0-060-12083-1

The Armed Man: A Mass for Peace
Complete full score
ISMN: 979-0-060-12255-2
Complete vocal score (SATB & piano)
ISMN: 979-0-060-11545-5
Choral suite vocal score (SATB & piano)
ISMN: 979-0-060-11410-6

Requiem
Vocal score (SATB & piano)
ISMN: 979-0-060-11684-1
Available separately:
Pie Jesu (SATB & piano)
ISMN: 979-0-060-11883-8
Pie Jesu (SSA & piano)
ISMN: 979-0-060-11887-6
Farewell
ISMN: 979-0-060-11886-9
Three Haikus (SATB & piano)
ISMN: 979-0-060-11888-3

Te Deum
Vocal score (SATB & piano)
ISMN: 979-0-060-12031-2

Adiemus I: Songs of Sanctuary
Full score
ISMN: 979-0-060-10887-7
Vocal score (SSAA & piano)
ISMN: 979-0-060-10374-2
Pack of ten vocal scores (SSAA & piano)
ISMN: 979-0-060-10501-2

Joy to the World
Vocal score (SATB & piano)
ISMN: 979-0-060-12217-0

Stella natalis
Vocal score (SATB & piano)
ISMN: 979-0-060-12216-3